AMERICAN WILDLIFE

Previous page: The buttressed mountains of Denali National Park in Alaska rise behind a bull moose, grazing on aquatic vegetation; moose often submerge completely when feeding this way. The Alaskan moose is the largest of four subspecies, including the Shiras moose of the Rocky Mountains.

2

Even in the fleeting alpine summer, few animals venture above the timberline. Grizzlies move into the high meadows to feed after a winter spent sleeping in a snug den. White-tailed ptarmigan, grouse-like birds that are year-round alpine residents, exchange one flawless camouflage for another, molting pure white winter plumage and growing new feathers that match the mottled rocks.

Other mountains have their own specialties. The slopes of the Cascades and Coastal Range holds herds of Columbian and Sitka black-tailed deer, subspecies of the more widespread mule deer. Black-tails live in the shady hardwood forests, and small herds will defend their territory from others—something related species of deer do not do. Roosevelt elk, found in the mountains of Olympic National Park in Washington, are a subspecies heavier and darker than elk elsewhere in the West; they range seasonally between the rain forests of the lowlands and the alpine tundra of the mountain summits. Where British Columbia and the Yukon meet at the northern end of the Rockies, bighorns are replaced by Stone's sheep, a variety with dark gray bodies and white heads—the least known of North America's wild sheep, in one of the continent's wildest places.

The Deserts

When the sun sets over the desert, and the scorching temperatures rapidly fall, a landscape that seemed empty by day comes alive.

Animals that sought refuge from the sun move out into the open. Rodents—pocket mice, wood rats, kangaroo rats and deer mice—scurry about, gleaning seeds, cactus fruits and invertebrates. They, in turn, are prey for skunks, rattlesnakes, kit foxes, coyotes, bobcats and other predators.

The cool, damp night breathes life back into the desert, but it cannot completely counter the hardships that animals must face in these crucibles of North America. To survive, wildlife has adapted itself to the demands of the desert.

Actually, there are three major deserts: the Great Basin, the Sonoran and the Chihuahuan; a fourth, the Mojave, is an intergrade between the Great Basin and Chihuahuan. Each desert has its own mix of wildlife, because each offers different living conditions.

The Sonoran is the "classic" desert, an expanse of sand and rock in southern California and Arizona that extends south through Mexico. By far, the Sonoran has the most variety of animals and plants of any of the U.S. deserts. Cacti grow in unimaginable diversity, from squat barrel cacti to the giant saguaro.

The Chihuahuan desert of west Texas and southern New Mexico is perhaps best exemplified by Big Bend National Park, along the Rio Grande River in Texas. The creosote bush grows everywhere in the park, filling the air with its strong odor. Scaled quail scurry among the prickly pear, one of this desert's abundant cacti.

While the Chihuahuan and Sonoran are so-called hot deserts, the Great Basin desert to the north is a "cold desert," because the majority of its precipitation falls as winter snow. Covering most of Nevada and parts of Utah, Washington and Idaho, the Great Basin has a paucity of life, especially when compared to the complex ecosystem in the Sonoran desert.

The deserts share many species of wild animals. Pronghorn, including the critically endangered Sonoran subspecies in Arizona, are able to survive on the poor forage, as are mule deer. In the Sonoran and Chihuahuan deserts, collared peccaries—small, wild pigs—move in tightly knit family groups, wary to an attack by predators. Red-tailed hawks, golden eagles and the uncommon Harris' hawk hunt rodents by day, while at night, great horned owls and the diminutive elf owl take to the air. Roadrunners endure the heat of day to catch lizards or snakes, including venomous species.

The rare kit fox shows some of the physical and behavioral adaptions to life in the desert. Fairly small, it has a greater surface area-to-body mass ratio than do foxes that live in cooler climates; for that reason, it is able to disperse its body heat more easily. Very large ears help cool the fox, as well as aid it in hunting rodents. During the day, the kit fox stays below ground, where the temperature is lower and the humidity is higher (in part because of the fox's respiration), thus cutting water loss.

Large ears are a common heat-reduction device among desert mammals. The black-tailed and antelope jackrabbits have the most outlandishly large ears, but the desert cottontail, cactus mouse and desert woodrat sport ears much bigger than closely related, cool-climate species.

Rain comes infrequently to the desert, but when a heavy, soaking downpour does occur, the dry landscape bursts with life and color. Seeds that may have waited years suddenly germinate. When spring rains hit the Sonora, the common image of a desert as empty sand is put spectacularly to rest, as blossoms of every shade spring forth.

Rainfall draws life from the ground in other ways. Spadefoot toads, usually cloistered underground in burrows, swarm to the surface for a frenzy of mating. In wetter regions of North America, an entire summer may pass between the time a toad's eggs are laid, and when the tadpoles change to toads and leave the water. But because a spadefoot toad doesn't have the luxury of time, its offspring go from eggs to land in less than two weeks. Even then, many die when pools dry up under the returning sun—the one harsh absolute in the desert.

Pinewoods and Swamps: The South

Three distinct regions, each with its own plants and animals, give the U.S. South a diversity of wildlife unmatched anywhere else in North America.

Along the coast, from Norfolk, Virginia to the southern tip of Texas, runs the great Coastal Plain—flat and humid, grown with loblolly and longleaf pine. Inland is the Piedmont, rolling hills of hardwoods and conifers that separate the Coastal Plain from the third major region, the Appalachian Mountains.

Much of the Coastal Plain is dominated by water—by the Atlantic Ocean and Gulf of Mexico, by saltwater marshes, freshwater swamps and the Everglades. Not surprisingly, the continent's greatest concentrations of waterbirds are found here, although their numbers have dropped precipitously in recent years due to changes in the natural flow of water. In southern Florida, mangrove trees rim the shore, sprouting from saltwater and supporting nesting colonies of brown pelicans. Limpkins, with their strange, crying call, hunt for snails in inland swamps.

The open pinelands of the Coastal Plain are home to an endangered species, the red-cockaded woodpecker, a ladder-backed bird that only chops its nest holes in pines infected with red-heart fungus. In the same forests lives Bachman's sparrow, a retiring species whose trilling call is heard more often than the singer is seen.

In the swamps of the Coastal Plain, from Virginia to the Florida panhandle, lives the marsh rabbit, a cottontail with most unrabbit-like habits. With its dark brown fur and gray tail, it looks terribly ordinary—until it takes to the water, for the marsh rabbit is an excellent swimmer, even hiding partly submerged when predators threaten. A larger cousin, the swamp rabbit of the Mississippi basin, is equally at home in water.

The Piedmont plateau of Georgia and the Carolinas, with its mixture of farms and hard-wood/conifer forests, is rich in wildlife—deer, red and gray fox, cardinals, bobwhites, wild tur-keys, opossums, Carolina chickadees and hundreds of other species. Unlike the Coastal Plain or the mountains, the Piedmont has few creatures uniquely its own, and in many ways, the wildlife is similar to that of the Northeast. Among the exceptions are brown-headed nuthatches (almost always found in stands of loblolly pine), chuck-will's-widows and blue grosbeaks.

The Blue Ridge Mountains provide a finger of New England that sticks deep into the South. On high, cool slopes, "northern" species like showshoe hares, Canada warblers, winter wrens, ravens and juncos find shelter in forests of pine, oak and maple.

The South has an abundance of rodents, some native and some newcomers. Marsh rice rats (also plentiful on interior wetlands), build round nests of reeds that they weave above the water on standing stalks. The cotton rat, an inhabitant of inland fields, is usually credited with being the most common mammal in the region.

Small and portly, the muskrat would attract little attention, were it not for its numbers and fur. With its chestnut-color guard hairs and plush coat of blue-gray underfur, a muskrat pelt has many uses in the fur industry, and millions are taken each year—most from the marshes of the South. In many rural areas, the winter economy depends to large degree on trapping, and musk-rats are the mainstay.

Sharing the marshes with the muskrat is a South American import, the nutria. Weighing 15 or 20 pounds, the nutria is considerably bigger than any muskrat, even though both species have the same general body shape for aquatic life. Originally raised on fur farms, nutrias escaped in the 1930s in Louisiana, multiplied and promptly ate their way across the South—and quickly wore out their welcome. An adult may eat three pounds of food each day, and where popula-tions are high, nutria can strip a marsh of its plant life.

The Everglades ecosystem of southern Florida—extending, in besieged parcels, far beyond its namesake national park—is unlike anything else on the continent. In pre-settlement days, a thin sheet of water flowed unobstructed over hundreds of miles of saw grass and forested islands, from Lake Okeechobee south in a gentle westward curve terminating in coastal mangrove swamps. This "river of grass" had its own schedule of rising and falling water levels, around which every one of its plants and animals timed their lives. In late winter, for instance, when the dry season traditionally reduced water levels and concentrated fish in shrinking pools, the abundant wading birds of the Everglades—herons, egrets, storks, ibises and spoonbills—had easy hunting, and could raise their chicks.

But Florida's successive booms—first agriculture, then housing—have strained the Everglades' delicate plumbing. Below Lake Okeechobee, vegetable and cane fields occupy much of what was the northern Everglades. Levees and dikes intercept the natural flow, even as storm run-off from the eastern coast metropolis floods into the 'Glades at unexpected intervals. The predictable waxing and waning of water has changed drastically, to the detriment of its wildlife. Drought in the 1960s, then decades of unusually high water, have seriously hurt some species; the endangered wood stork has dropped from tens of thousands of pairs in the 1920s to only a few thousand in the entire Southeast.

That is not to suggest that the Everglades are barren. With about 300 species of birds, as well as deer, bear, bobcat, raccoon, otter, alligator, eastern diamondback rattlesnakes, multitudes of frogs, toads, turtles and lizards, it is a showcase of subtropical wildlife. Flocks of pink roseate spoonbills, with their outlandish beaks, nest in the mangroves. Rarest of the rare, a handful of Florida panthers roam the palmetto thickets, the last of a population of swamp cats that were once found throughout the region. Only in the Everglades is their scream heard today, a vestige of wildness in a vast and grassy wilderness.

Fastest of North America's land animals, a pronghorn antelope, like this fine buck, can hit 50 miles per hour in short bursts, and can sustain runs at lesser speeds for miles. Once more common than even the great bison herds, pronghorns suffered badly at the hands of settlers and market hunters. Today, though, nearly a quarter million roam the western prairies, and they are a common sight in Wyoming and Montana.

Strictly a nighttime hunter, this desert kit fox spends its days below ground, in its burrow. As with jackrabbits, the overly large ears are an adaptation to the hot desert environment, radiating away the fox's body heat. Rather small as foxes go, the kit fox preys on mice, insects, birds and lizards.

Huddled against the tundra, an arctic fox shows the blue-gray
fur its kind wear during the brief northern summer. The dark
fur is replaced in winter by a camouflaging coat of white. An
efficient predator, the arctic fox is not above scavenging—a
beached whale has been known to attract them by the hundreds.

Following Page: With Glacier National Park's
mountains for a spectacular backdrop, this mountain
goat feeds among spruce trees near an alpine
lake. When the winter snows bury such forage, the
goat may be forced to subsist on lichens that grow
on windswept cliffs.

Eastern box turtles, like this red-eyed male, are omnivorous, eating a wide variety of insects, worms, fruits and berries. A hinge across the plastron, or lower shell, allows the box turtle to pull its head and legs safely inside.

A muffled snore in the swamp is usually a clue that the leopard frogs are breeding, for the calls of courting males sounds little like the croak most people expect. Several closely related species are found from the arctic to Mexico, but all carry the distinct back spots.

With the assurance of a tightrope artist, a green treefrog clings
to a twig, aided by adhesive discs at the end of each toe.
Many treefrogs, including the green in the South and the spring
peeper in the North, can change color, but the phenomenon is
involuntary, ruled by temperature and the frog's physical
condition.

As a group, lizards seem to be less tolerant of cool climates than their fellow reptiles, the snakes and turtles. Most of North America's lizard species are found in the West and Southwest, although a handful do range into southern New England.

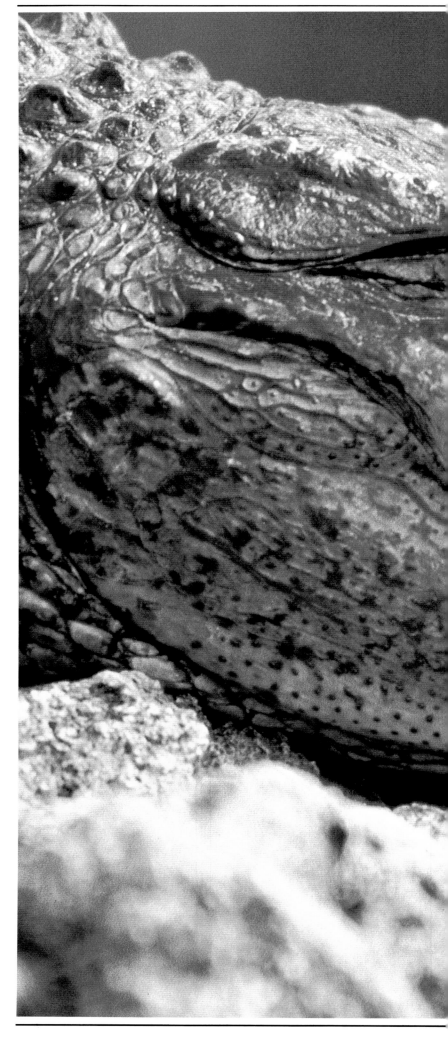

Armor-plated but agile, alligators are members of an ancient
order of reptiles, the crocodilians. Alligators are found almost
exclusively in freshwater, while the much rarer American
crocodile prefers salt or brackish water.

Following Page: Water cascades from the antlers of
a bull moose, belly-deep in a pond. The "bell," a
pendulous, fur-covered flap of skin beneath the
throat, is larger in bulls than in cows and serves a
function as yet undeciphered by science.

Intelligent, adaptable and by turns endearing and exasperating, raccoons occupy almost every habitat in North America, from western shorelines to Florida swamps and Canadian forests. In suburbs, raccoons can be as common as barbecue grills, and they can live nicely in city alleys, raiding garbage cans for food.

As dusty brown as the Texas brush, two collared peccaries, or javelinas, pick their way through Big Bend National Park. The only native wild pig in North America, peccaries live in small herds, marking their territory with a powerful musk.

Habitue of forests almost everywhere, the gray squirrel is one of the most familiar of the continent's mammals. The eastern gray squirrel ranges from woodlots in the Great Plains to the Atlantic, while the somewhat larger western gray is found in California, Washington and Oregon.

In the fall, pronghorn bucks gather harems of does, like this
small herd on the Montana prairie. While the mating season
lasts, the buck will defend his harem against intruding males,
ensuring that the fawns born the next spring will have been
sired by the most vigorous bucks.

The scene is a common one almost everywhere in the East: a cottontail rabbit framed by grass still wet from the preceding night's dew. In other parts of the country, closely related species—some so similar that only experts can tell them apart—replace the eastern cottontail.

With winter already dusting Mount Washington with snow, maples in New Hampshire's White Mountains reveal a last blush of red before dropping their leaves. The Northeast is a melting pot for animals and plants of both the north, like the loon, and the south, like the opossum.

America, swamping that continent's unique wildlife and apparently forcing many into extinction through increased competition.

Taken in sum, the immigrations gave North America a rich variety of animals by the beginning of the last glacial period, the Wisconsin, some 10,000 years ago. Modern species were in evidence—brown and black bears, elk, moose, muskoxen, bison and caribou. But that wasn't all. The Pleistocene is best known for its "megafauna," mammals of enormous size: short-faced bears much larger than grizzlies; long-horned bison; mastodons and mammoths; ground sloths 15 feet long; saber-toothed cats preying on herds of horses and camels; beavers many times the size of the modern species; giant wolves and cave lions. In a cold world, large size is a distinct advantage, because there is more heat-generating body mass in relation to heat-dispersing surface area. The principle can, incidentally, be seen at work today in many mammals; the Key deer of Florida are less than half the size of white-tailed deer in Maine.

The long canine teeth of the saber-toothed cats have raised more questions than there are answers for. There were a number of species of two distinct types, but all had fangs that were flattened in cross-section, with unpleasantly jagged tips. All in all, the teeth were impressive weaponry, but were so long that it is doubtful the cats could open their mouths far enough to actually bite, begging the question of function. One school of thought suggests the cats stabbed with closed mouths, rather than biting their victims. Other specialists, noting the high number of saber-toothed cat fossils with degenerative bone diseases, have forwarded the theory that they were carrion eaters—an idea that neatly sidesteps why a scavenger needs long fangs in the first place.

Just as there were two groups of saber-toothed cats with separate ancestry, prehistoric North America's bears came from different bloodlines. The great short-faced bear, which lingered through the end of the Pleistocene, died without evolutionary heirs, but two other groups were luckier. At an early stage of evolution, well before the ice age, the bear line split. One branch, through a slim-skull ancestor named *Ursus etruscus*, gave rise to brown bears and their strictly European ice-age cousin, the cave bears, including the North American species and the sun bear of Asia.

More recently—in fact, probably only since the tail end of the last ice age—polar bears evolved from brown bear stock. So dissimilar to the human eye, brown and polar bears are quite close genetically, and freely interbreed in captivity, producing fertile offspring. It seems likely that the rapid evolution of the polar bear came about only when the ice sheet had retreated enough to free the Arctic Ocean on a seasonal basis, setting up an ecosystem rich in marine life that a sea-going bear could exploit.

Then as now, wild animals lived at the whim of their environment. When the glaciers advanced, the biting cold would spread far down into North America, and muskoxen, mammoths and other tundra dwellers lived in what is now the mild Midwest. Further south, boreal forests held moose and mastodons. Eventually the glaciers would retreat, and species that had taken refuge in the south would follow the greening land north.

It was during the Wisconsin glaciation, when the Bering land bridge was again above the waves, that man first appeared in North America. As with the dispersal of the carnivores, it is certain that these Paleolithic hunters did not know they were setting foot on a new continent. They were simply following the herds, expanding generation by generation into fresh hunting grounds.

The impact of primitive hunters, in small numbers and using only spears, would be predictably small. And yet, the appearance of people in North America coincided with the wave of extinctions that blotted out most of the megafauna.

The great Pleistocene extinctions, roughly 10,000 years ago, remain unexplained. Lost were the biggest and most spectacular of North America's mammals—the mammoths, mastodons and ground sloths, cave lions, glyptodonts, long-horned bison and short-faced bears. Lost too were ten of the eleven species of pronghorns, and the horses and camels that evolved in North America.

Again, the question is why. Why extinction on such a sweeping scale? Some experts have advanced the theory of a "Pleistocene overkill," claiming that humans fouled up the delicate balance of ice age ecology, hunting the megafaunal grazers into extinction and robbing their predators of food. Another theory is that, with the close of the Wisconsin glaciation, the dry, cold climate of the tundra and plains was replaced with one substantially wetter; unable to cope with mounting snowfalls, the theory goes, many species died out. Still another guess comes from the steadily decreasing size of some megafauna members in the waning days of the ice age. The evolution of mammoths into dwarf forms, for instance, is seen as evidence that the species were losing genetic viability.

The mystery is unlikely to be solved any time soon, if at all, but the results cannot be disputed: with the close of the Wisconsin glaciation and the mass extinction, the composition of North America's modern wildlife had been largely determined.

It is common to speak of the ice ages as something of the past, but that may be short-sighted. This may be nothing more than another period of glacial retreat, following the pattern of those in previous millennia. As the Wisconsin ice sheet melted, the arctic conditions in the continental heartland eased. Tundra was replaced by grasslands, then by boreal forests, then by hardwoods as the climate warmed. The process is not yet complete; along the Alaskan coast, the ice is still in retreat, and the forest is recolonizing glaciated areas at a rate of several miles a century. Bones suggest that moose once lived in Pennsylvania, but they had vanished into New York and Canada by the time the first white settlers arrived.

Within the past 150 years, many southern animals have been made surprising advances into the north. Armadillos were unknown north of the Rio Grande before 1880, but within a century (and with a fair bit of human help) they made their way through Texas, Louisiana and Florida. Opossums, once confined below the Mason-Dixon line, now show their toothy grins clear to southern Canada. Birdwatchers chart the steady, northward advance of mockingbirds and cardinals over much the same territory. Turkey vultures have pushed into Quebec and Ontario, while the more southerly black vulture now breeds in Pennsylvania and New York, leap-frogging into new territory every year or two.

It is usually assumed that human changes in the environment, like the clearing of the eastern forests, were the reasons for these incursions. While that may be true, people have a tendency to see themselves at the core of everything. Nature is never static, and such range expansions may owe as much to a continuation of post-glacial recovery as to human meddling.

Besides the lakes and ice-carved mountains, the glaciers left a living legacy in their wake. On the mountaintops of the Appalachians, curving far in the Deep South, are "biological islands."

As mentioned, the ice sheets stopped in New York and the Great Lakes, but their influence extended much farther south, in the form of cold temperatures. Such a climate favors coniferous trees, and thus much of the South had forests of cool-weather softwoods like red spruce, firs and hemlocks. When the glaciers retreated, the climate mellowed and hardwoods returned, confining these conifers increasingly to the mountains.

Today, on the highest ridges of the Appalachians, these ice age forests remain, still supporting wildlife representative of areas far to the north—snowshoe hares, red squirrels, ravens, redbacked voles, winter wrens, ruffed grouse and golden-crowned kinglets, among others. The same phenomenon occurs to the north as well; boreal chickadees, spruce grouse and gray-cheeked thrushes live in the Adirondack highlands of New York, far south of their usual Canadian range.

In the Appalachians, many ridges and damp glens have been cut off from each other by a sea of warm, dry lowlands for thousands of years, resulting in the sort of isolation that permits rapid evolution. The Appalachian woodland salamander is a case in point. Early herpetologists, exploring the damp mountainsides and cataloging their finds, discovered a staggering variety of lungless *Plethodon* salamanders. The Metcalf's salamander was plain gray, the Clemson's was marbled in greenish brown. Salamanders with red cheeks were obviously different than those with red legs—and so on. Each new find was accorded the status of a separate species. Not until recently, with more study, has it been learned that these "species" are really closely related forms of the same creature, the Appalachian woodland salamander.

Whether in the eastern hills or the Southwestern desert, a sharp buzz from the underbrush is a warning that is not to be ignored, for rattlesnakes have adapted to most habitats from the Canadian border south.

Threatened by danger, many snakes (and a few lizards) will vibrate their tails, and in dry leaves the result is disconcerting, to say the least. But if there are no leaves around, or if they are wet and silent, the gambit is less effective. With its rattles, the rattlesnake has removed chance from the equation.

The rattle itself is nothing more than an overlapping series of scaly buttons, loosely joined one to the next. When the snake vibrates its tail, the buttons make a dry, insectlike buzz as they rub against each other.

The old saw about judging a rattler's age by the number of buttons is false. A newborn has only one, but quickly adds more as it grows and sheds its skin—something that can happen several times a summer. In addition, the rattles are fragile, and buttons are often torn free when the snake crawls through rocks or dense brush.

What is remarkable about the rattle is that the rattler itself can't hear its own noise. Like all snakes, they are deaf to airborne vibrations. If anything, this demonstrates the unplanned nature of evolution; it is common to say "the rattlesnake developed rattles," but it was hardly a conscious idea on the snake's part. Rattle development had far more to do with the hard hooves of prairie grazers.

A rattlesnake packs twin venom glands in its head, with a sophisticated system of hollow, pivoting fangs to deliver it. Although primarily used to kill small mammals upon which it feeds, a rattlesnake can use its venom to deadly effect for protection—against a single animal. A fox that gets too close can be bitten, and the searing pain from the venom will certainly chase it away.

But a fast-moving herd of animals is a different matter completely. A rattlesnake may bite the first individual in the herd, and perhaps even the second, but the tide of bison will thunder over the hapless snake a second later, mashing it into the ground. The snake needs some way of warning the herd away. Bright colors might work, but they are a constant advertisement, and there are many predators that willingly feed on rattlers. Much better is an auditory warning that can be used only when needed.

And so, it seems, was the rattle born. Since most snakes vibrate their tails anyway, it is not hard to imagine how, through natural selection, some with loose scales at the tip would be capable of making more noise—and thus stand a better chance of surviving to reproduce. (That might also explain why an island-bound species in the Gulf of California has lost its rattles.)

Rattlesnakes belong to a group of strictly New World reptiles knows as pit vipers, named for heat-sensitive organs between the eye and nostril. Each pit has two chambers, separated by a thin membrane, and can detect subtleties of temperature as little as a single degree. Although their effective range is only a foot or two, the pits allow a snake to follow its prey in total darkness. Copperheads and cottonmouths are also pit vipers, but rattlesnakes are by far the most common representatives of the group, with about 15 species. They range in size from the massive eastern diamondback, at as much as eight feet, to the diminutive pygmy rattlesnakes of the South, scarcely 20 inches long.

There are two major kinds of snake venom. Southern coral snakes, like their Old World relatives the cobras, have venom that attacks the nervous system. Pit vipers carry hemotoxic venom, a pale, yellowish liquid made up primarily of enzymes that assail blood vessels and cells.

When a rattlesnake strikes at a rodent, it aims for the animal's forequarters. As it lunges, the snake opens its mouth wide, causing its fangs to swing from the roof of its mouth into a vertical, locked position. On impact, muscles inject a heavy dose of venom through the hollow fangs into the prey. An instant later, the snake pulls back, to wait for the venom to work.

A pit viper bite is intensely painful. The venom immediately begins breaking down the cellular structure around the bite, even as the victim's bloodstream spreads the venom through its body. In a small animal, death usually comes quickly, from internal bleeding and heart failure. Only then will the snake eat.

Flight, not hunting, is the end-all and be-all of a hummingbird's existence. Other birds fly faster or higher, but none can match a hummingbird's acrobatic skills—diving, twisting, flipping, hovering and even backing up. There are more than 300 species of this New World group, most living in their native South America. A few, however, have colonized North America. The ruby-throated hummingbird is found across the East, and the rufous hummingbird of the West has even penetrated far up the coast into Alaska. But the greatest variety are found in the Southwest, in mountain canyons and stream valleys, where they flit like gems among the flowers.

Hummingbirds are all built along the same basic lines—a long beak and tongue for sipping nectar, thin, pointed wings and tiny, almost useless legs. The females of most North American species are virtually indistinguishable from each other, with green backs and white breasts, but the males glisten with color. The violet-crowned hummingbird has a red bill and iridescent purple head. The magnificent hummingbird sports a vivid green throat gorget, the Anna's, a head wrapped in rose-red feathers. The male rufous hummingbird is almost completely red, with a green crown and an orange gorget. Unlike the feathers of a robin, which get their color from pigment in the feather cells, the red in a ruby-throated hummingbird's gorget owes its brilliance to the feather's structure, which fractures sunlight and bounces red wavelengths to the viewer's eye. At the wrong angle, the gorget can appear black.

Specialized body structure allows a hummer to pull off amazing aerial maneuvers. Its humerus (the upper "arm" bone) is very short, leaving most of the wing supported by bones analagous to a human's fingers. The elbow and wrist joints are almost fused for greater support, but the shoulder joint rotates freely, allowing the wing to pivot in almost any direction. Considering its tiny size, the breastbone has a deep keel, to anchor powerful chest muscles that move the wings.

Birds of any sort are active, but hummingbirds take it to the extreme, burning up calories at such a rate that they must feed on sugar-rich nectar and insects every few minutes throughout the day. The heartbeat of a resting turkey is 93 per minute, that of a hummingbird, more than 1,200. Hummers, in fact, have probably the highest metabolism of any vertebrate animal. Maintaining such ferocious energy consumption through a chilly night would be impossible, so many hummingbirds in cool climates enter a sort of dormancy at sunset. The blue-throated hummingbird of southeastern Arizona is one species prone to such torpors. Its heartbeat has been known to drop from 1,260 beats per minute during daytime flights to only 36 per minute at night.

The diversity of North America's wildlife continues to grow. Man has added to it, intentionally and otherwise, by transplanting animals from other continents. But sometimes, the animals are capable of making the trip themselves, as cattle egrets have proved.

On the African savannah, cattle egrets are a common sight, walking beneath rhinos and elephants, grabbing insects the huge beasts flush. In the late 1800s, a few showed up on the eastern coast of South America, probably shoved off course by powerful trade winds, which blow east-to-west in the Southern Hemisphere.

Birds are blown off-course all the time; such "accidentals" lend birdwatching much of its spice. Most are unable to adapt to their new environment and die.

The wayward cattle egrets did not die.

Far from it, they prospered, spreading rapidly up through Central America. In 1952, seven were found in Florida. A decade later, cattle egrets were found in virtually every U.S. state, and had become the most common North American egret. The cattle egret explosion continues today, although at a slower rate, because the species seems to be reaching its northern limits.

One of the reasons the cattle egret did so well is that the ecological niche it occupies—catching insects, amphibians and small animals in agricultural land—was not being filled by native species. All of North America's wading birds prefer wetlands, and although cattle egrets accept such habitats as well, they have a flexibility native species lack.

The cattle egret is the most dramatic example of natural colonization, but there are many more. The common black-headed gull of Europe and Iceland routinely shows up, in small numbers, along the East Coast. It has bred for a number of years in Canada, and has begun to expand south along the shore. Gulls, with their nautical habits and strong flight, are prime candidates for accidental transplantation. Lesser black-backed gulls and little gulls, both European, now breed along the East Coast and Great Lakes respectively, and Ross' gull of Siberia has recently started to nest in arctic Canada.

A glance at field guides for North America, northern European and northern Asian birds reveals the homogeneity of the Northern Hemisphere's birdlife—and a glance at the map shows why. Between Siberia and the Aleutian Islands are but a few miles of water, and the Canadian Maritimes, Greenland, Iceland and Scotland provide way stations for hop-scotching flyers. Birds with the bad luck to be caught in strong winds (or to be born with a miscalibrated sense of direction) are forever landing where they are not supposed to be, and over thousands of years, some have made the move successfully. In particular, many species of ducks, gulls, terns, shorebirds and auks show up on both sides of the Atlantic. Often, the only difference is the name: an oldsquaw in the United States is a long-tailed duck in England, a common merganser here is a goosander there. Otherwise the species are identical.

Flying north from the tropics each spring, more than 50 species of wood warblers inundate the forests of North America with color and song. Aptly called the "butterflies of the bird world," warblers are the most beautiful family on the continent, sporting varied patterns of yellows, oranges, blues, grays, greens, reds and every hue in between. They look as though they would be more at home in a rain forest than a New England woodlot, but warblers (unlike hummingbirds) evolved in North America. Biologists guess that after the last glacial retreat, warblers began probing up from the South, breeding in the boreal forests where insect life is abundant. As the forests moved farther into Canada, succeeding generations of warblers followed, returning over ever-greater distances to their winter homes. Today, warblers are found most commonly in eastern Canada, although species have adapted to almost every forested habitat on the continent.

Songbirds, with their weaker flying abilities and overland migration routes, have less chance of surviving a transoceanic hop, so North America's smaller birds tend to be unique to the Western Hemisphere. As with every rule, there are a few exceptions. By tracing migratory paths, ornithologists have been able to determine that several arctic birds are relatively recent additions to North America—and they can see how at least one native bird is branching out into another continent.

Arctic warblers are members of an Old World family and are, despite the name, more closely related to thrushes than to wood warblers. In North America, this small, plain species is found in western and interior Alaska, which it apparently colonized from Siberia. Each fall, rather than flying south, U.S. arctic warblers cross the Bering Strait, flock with Siberian birds and migrate to Southeast Asia. Another Siberian species, the bluethroat, has also made the leap into Alaska, moving to Africa for the winter.

The northern wheatear, yet another thrush, has taken a two-pronged approach. One population of wheatears has expanded from Europe and Iceland into the eastern arctic, while a different population has taken the Siberia-Alaska route. Come winter, the Alaskan birds fly west and the eastern birds fly east, but both groups eventually meet on their ancestral African wintering grounds.

The pectoral sandpiper is a cardinal-sized shorebird that breeds in two distinct populations—along the coastal fringe of the Arctic Ocean and Hudson Bay, and in Siberia. Which came first? Apparently the North American birds; Siberian pectorals fly east across the Bering Strait and join those from Canada and Alaska before moving on to South America, a reverse of the arctic warbler's migration. In the intercontinental exchange of species, turnabout is apparently fair play.

As is the case for many predators, female bobcats have fairly
small territories, while males are more nomadic, hunting
over much wider areas that encompass the ranges of up to a
half-dozen females. Mating occurs in late winter, after which
this most common of North American wild cats resumes its
solitary ways.

**Following Page: This dam of logs and mud shows
why the beaver enjoys an unmatched reputation as
an engineer, and as the only North American animal
that, like people, changes its environment to suit
itself. By damming a stream or river, the beaver
floods surrounding forests, providing itself with a
handy food supply and the safety of deep water.**

Light glints off the shells of painted turtles, sunning themselves amid blooming spatterdock in a New England lake. Because they lack an internal mechanism to control their body temperature, all reptiles, including turtles, must move from sun to shade many times during the day. If too cold, they become torpid and slow; if too hot, they may quickly succumb to heat stroke and die.

A closeup of a snapping turtle shows the sharp, powerful beak that this species uses to great advantage to eat fish, carrion and even ducks. While the strength of a snapper's jaws has been exaggerated by popular myth (it cannot, for instance, sever a finger with a single bite), those who hunt snappers for their meat have a healthy respect for them.

In the dimly lit world of a Florida reef, fish school beneath the concealing branches of elkhorn coral, itself a colony of tiny animals. Coral reefs occur only in coastal areas with warm, clear seawater, and are astounding in the complexity and beauty of life they hold.

Cupped to catch the slightest sound, the black-rimmed ears of cautious mule deer zero in on the photographer. Also known as burro deer because of their ears, mule deer inhabit most of the West, from the Great Plains to the Pacific coast, traveling between mountain pastures in summer and lowlands in the winter.

Backlit by a scorching Texas sun, a black-tailed jackrabbit's enormous ears show the network of blood vessels that allow the hare's body heat to dissipate—a function which, in the desert, is just as important to the jackrabbit as hearing. Black-taileds are among the West's most common small mammals; two other species, the white-tailed and antelope jackrabbit, have more restricted ranges.

The sunlight of a winter's day in Ontario sparkles off the coat of a red squirrel, foraging for food beneath snow-covered logs. Red squirrels are the busybodies of the northern woods, scolding humans and predators from the safety of the trees while alerting the forest that danger is near.

Largest of all the world's deer, a moose like this Alaskan bull may weigh as much as 1,600 pounds and carry palmated antlers that span six feet. Creatures of the swampy muskeg and thick spruce forests, moose are found in a wide band from Alaska and the Rocky Mountains across most of Canada to Maine.

Holding tight, two baby opossums hitch a ride on their mother's back. Litters are normally much larger. A persistent myth about opossums—one of many that this odd animal has inspired—claims that the female arches her tail over her back so her babies may dangle by their own tails from it.